MEN 59372091833718

WITHDRAWN

WORN, SOILED, OBSOLETE

D0609448

CONOZCO LOS COLORES
I KNOW COLORS

By Mary Rose Osburn
Traducido por Fátima Rateb

Gareth Stevens
PUBLISHING

conceptos
básicos

Conozco muchos colores.
El auto es rojo.

I know many colors.
The car is red.

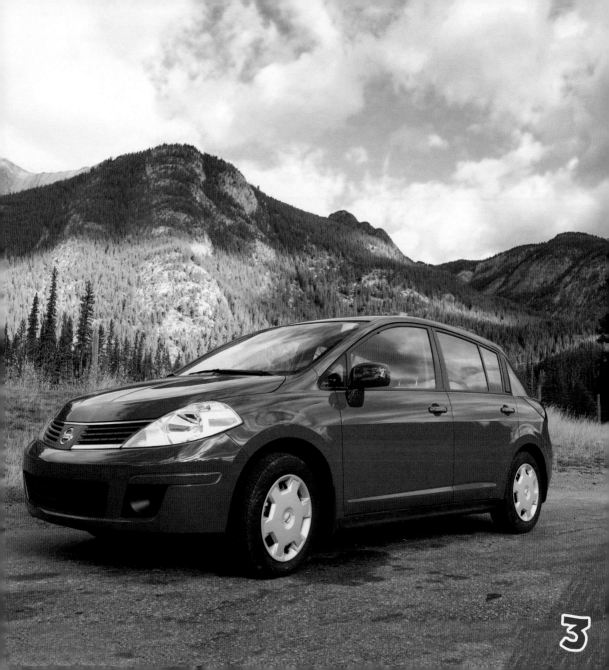

La gorra es naranja.

The hat is orange.

4

5

El plátano es amarillo.

The banana is yellow.

7

El dinosaurio es verde.

The dinosaur is green.

9

El tobogán es azul.

The slide is blue.

11

El oso es marrón.

The bear is brown.

13

El globo es morado.

The balloon is purple.

14

15

El gato es negro.

The cat is black.

17

El perro es blanco.

- -

The dog is white.

18

19

La cebra es
negra y blanca.

The zebra is
black and white.

21

¡Un arcoíris es
de muchos colores!
¿Qué colores conoces?

A rainbow is
many colors!
What colors
do you know?

23

Please visit our website, www.garethstevens.com. For a free color catalog of all our high-quality books, call toll free 1-800-542-2595 or fax 1-877-542-2596.

Cataloging-in-Publication Data

Names: Osburn, Mary Rose.
Title: I know colors = Conozco los colores / Mary Rose Osburn.
Description: New York : Gareth Stevens Publishing, 2017. | Series: What I know = Lo que conozco | In English and Spanish
Identifiers: ISBN 9781482461978 (library bound)
Subjects: LCSH: Color–Juvenile literature.
Classification: LCC QC495.5 O83 2017 | DDC 535.6–dc23

First Edition

Published in 2017 by
Gareth Stevens Publishing
111 East 14th Street, Suite 349
New York, NY 10003

Copyright © 2017 Gareth Stevens Publishing

Translator: Fátima Rateb
Editorial Director, Spanish: Nathalie Beullens-Maoui
Editor, English: Therese Shea
Designer: Sarah Liddell

Photo credits: Cover, p. 1 (stripes) Eky Studio/Shutterstock.com; cover, p. 1 (crayons) daizuoxin/Shutterstock.com; p. 3 Stephen McSweeny/Shutterstock.com; p. 5 kokanphoto/Shutterstock.com; p. 7 mmkarabella/Shutterstock.com; p. 9 iMaksymPhoto/Shutterstock.com; p. 11 MaxyM/Shutterstock.com; p. 13 Canon Boy/Shutterstock.com; p. 15 Mike Flippo/Shutterstock.com; p. 17 Suvorov_Alex/Shutterstock.com; p. 19 Mark Herreid/Shutterstock.com; p. 21 Attila JANDI/Shutterstock.com; p. 23 Preto Perola/Shutterstock.com.

All rights reserved. No part of this book may be reproduced in any form without permission in writing from the publisher, except by a reviewer.

Printed in the United States of America

CPSIA compliance information: Batch #CW17GS: For further information contact Gareth Stevens, New York, New York at 1-800-542-2595.